The Book of
101
Thoughts

The Book of
101
Thoughts

**Master Your Mind
and
Conquer Your World**

David Andrew

101 Book of Thoughts

Copyright© David Andrew

All rights reserved. No part of this book may be reproduced in any form by photocopying or any electronic or mechanical means, including information storage or retrieval systems, without permission in writing from both the copyright owner and the publisher of the book. The right of David Andrew to be identified as the author of this work has been asserted by him in accordance with the Copyright, Designs and Patents Act 1988 and any subsequent amendments thereto. A catalogue record for this book is available from the British Library.

All Scripture Quotations have been taken from the NIV

ISBN: 978-1-911697-62-6

1st Edition by Kingdom Publishers, London, UK.

You can purchase copies of this book from any leading bookstore or email contact@kingdompublishers.co.uk

"For as a man thinketh in his heart so is he"
Proverbs 23:7

The Book of 101 Thoughts is a book that will make you reflect on your life, and if you would like to reflect and improve on matters in your own life, then this is a book for you!

I got to know David Andrew through the many emails and telephone conversations we have had over the past six months. He is a man that is passionate about two things: Jesus and helping people reach unfulfilled areas in their lives.

Having read David's book 'The Book of 101 Thoughts', David goes into everyday areas of human lives and gives deep insights and revelations on how we should think about certain things from a Christian's perspective. My favourite is when David asks, *'Are we a fan or a follower of Jesus?'* There, David highlights the difference between the two and makes one think about what they are.

Another of David's great insights is about doublemindedness, and this happens with many Christians where they sit on the fence. Here David again explains what the Bible says about sitting on the wall and the dangers of being lukewarm as a Christian. So, David has taken essential scriptures from the word of God and teaches us to apply them in our daily lives.

I am recommending this book because there isn't another current book on the market that captures this attempt to transform our thinking by relating it to the word of God the way David has.

Pastor Maria Yiangou, Senior Pastor of Victory in Christ Ministries, London, UK

PREFACE

October 2009, early autumn, I boarded a British Airways direct flight from London Heathrow to Shanghai, China, on my first business trip. I felt good about myself, and this would be the start to fulfil my ambition of eventually being a millionaire. But nothing was further from the truth.

I was in a country where I did not speak or understand the native language. I was dependent on a Chinese person 95% of the time to assist me. After the initial shock of the sounds, smells, and people, I gathered myself. My business associate pleasantly greeted me in English with a smile. She quickly recognised me as the only Indian guy on the morning 8.30 a.m. flight. I also spotted her quickly among the sea of Chinese faces as she stood with my name placard in her hand. It made me feel a bit important because having travelled for years, I also dreamt of being received by someone with my name placard one day. Simultaneously I felt excited and anxious, not knowing how things would turn out.

As someone said, you never know what's around the corner and how true it was for me. Never in a million years I would have known that one visit to China and one person could radically change my life and turn my world upside down forever; it did!

As I was trying to rebuild a life, I realised I had swayed so far from the truth, my values, and guiding principles by surrendering to suppressed emotions, temptations like a cracked egg.

I gave in by deafening my conscience. The impact was catastrophic, like a seismic earthquake uprooting the world of my family life, sending tremors of shockwaves and pain to people in my orbit. The aftermath at the time I felt was irreparable, and I could never pull myself together again. The punishment felt like double jeopardy. As a day, months and years passed, among many lessons learnt, one that stood out most was that the grass might look greener on the other side of the fence, but a closer look revealed it needs regular mowing and everything else to keep it looking green. I realised there wasn't a lawnmower and no grass to mow and wandered in a parched land.

Fast forward, fourteen years in remaking a critical lesson I learnt. *Making mistakes and learning lessons go hand in hand.* It's crucial never to forget about learning from mistakes. Some mistakes are potentially disastrous without being given a second chance. There wasn't a second chance, and I had blown it, and no amount of begging would make a difference. I had to rebuild life from scratch and did not know where to start and where it would lead. The adage I hold dearly to this day; *Prevention is better than cure*, and it applies to all areas of life's wellbeing.

God promises from His word. The Lord says, "I will give you back what you lost to the swarming locusts, the hopping locusts, the stripping locusts, and the cutting locusts. It was I who sent this great destroying army against you." Joel 2:25

The Book of 101 Thoughts stems from lessons I learned and how they changed my thinking relatable to most people on an everyday practical level. My holistic way of thinking encapsulates my transformational journey. *I describe it as darkness to light, uncertainty to certainty, fear to faith and discouragement to empowerment.*

Our brain is a complex masterpiece emitting powerful emotions we can harness through critical thinking and emotional intelligence.

Everyone has their worldview. We live in a free-thinking world where we express our opinions. In this book, I have expressed mine and initiated curiosity, helping you explore your paradigms.

I hope to leave a world where my family and community can feel safe, blossom, and enjoy. The change began with me, and I hope it starts with you.

DEDICATION

I dedicate this book to my late parents, James, and Eleanor Andrew, who continues to be a source of inspiration that transformed my life.

My two handsome sons, James and Matthew, I am proud of how they grew into responsible men, kind and caring to their families and respectable citizens of the UK.

My two beautiful granddaughters, Mia and Chloe, are very young and a delight to all of us. They are talented and demonstrate a remarkable ability to comprehend and articulate their thoughts.

ACKNOWLEDGEMENT

I am thankful to my siblings, Smita, Melika and Nivesh, for their love and support. Demographically we live thousands of miles away, but our genuine love and care bond us together. They are a continuous source of help and encouragement to me.

I am grateful and proud of my beautiful six nieces and three nephews. As they are growing amid a rapidly changing world, I pray they will stay ahead of the game and aspire to gain wisdom to successfully navigate life and be a beacon of positive influence on their friends and community.

I am thankful to my wife, Yuqin (Sandy), who, within the last decade and to this day, continues to support me with her insights encouraging me to excel and succeed in my ventures.

I could list numerous people who supported and inspired me in their ways over the years. I am very grateful to all of them, especially to my two friends, Dinesh Mistry and Len Hardy, who stood by me during my life's darkest hours without criticism or judgment. And importantly,

I am very grateful to my life and business coaches, mentors, and friends for playing their part in bouncing off my ideas and guiding me to stay focused and on track to achieve my goals successfully. And amongst the coaches, two are Lana Maher, and Arikah Gamble encouraged and inspired me in writing this book.

Finally, my journey to living a transformative life wouldn't be possible without the significant help and critical source of spiritual strength and inspiration from God, my Heavenly Father, my saviour Jesus Christ and my silent guide, The Holy Spirit.

Cumulatively the support I received throughout my life, for which I am grateful, provokes me to think, "No man is an Island" We need each other!

FOREWORD

My name is Brian Hilliard, and as an author of 7 Books and Speaker since 2001, I've had the pleasure to know David Andrew for four years. Our relationship harmoniously grew professionally and as friends.

We first met through LinkedIn, and during that time, we've had a chance to grow and learn together through our work.

What I like about David, and why I'd encourage just about everyone to read this book, is his peace, balance and quiet confidence that underlies everything he does.

Many times, you see authors and coaches relentlessly trying to make a "name" for themselves, losing track of what coaching is all about…helping others through your experience.

David gets that 100%!

Not only does he help others officially as a Coach & Author, and his kindness is beyond just about anyone I know. But that wasn't always the case.

According to David, he used to be the tense, critical and not pleasant guy to be around. But through his work in this world and with the Lord, David experienced a rebirth to become the man he is today.

And it's through this book that he has been able to articulate the learnings and insights he learned along the way.

So if you're looking for more peace, harmony and contentment in your life, then "101 Thoughts - Master Your Mind and Conqueror Your World" I highly recommend you to read as it will help you self-reflect, evoking you to think about how you perceive the world around you.

PAGE OF CONTENT

Category	Insight Number
BUSINESS acumen	23, 75, 89, 99, 137, 143, 151, 209, 211, 217
ENVIRONMENT our relation to it	203, 205, 207
MINDSET growth	25, 29, 49, 51, 53, 63, 71, 85, 97, 107, 109, 111, 113, 115, 127, 133, 139, 145, 149, 159, 169, 173, 179, 185, 189, 193, 197, 223, 225, 229, 233
PRACTICAL daily living	27, 31, 37, 39, 69, 73, 77, 93, 101, 103, 117, 121, 123, 129, 141, 147, 155, 163, 175, 183, 199, 201, 219, 221, 227
RELATIONSHIP Values	79, 81, 105, 177
SPIRITUAL awareness	21, 35, 43, 47, 55, 57, 59, 61, 65, 95, 119, 135, 153, 157, 161, 165, 171, 181, 187, 191, 195, 215, 231, 235
SOCIAL our role in the society	33, 83, 87, 91, 125, 131, 213

DAVID ANDREW

YOUR THOUGHTS:

SPIRITUAL

1. **What is the difference between a fan and a follower of Jesus? A fan is like a sheep and may wander off to better pasture. A follower learns, grows, helps, and empowers others to follow.**

Being born and raised in a Christian family, I did not have a complete grasp of Christianity, except if I don't follow the path, I will end up in hell, but I will go to heaven if I do. Later I learned about my skewed view of Christianity, including the doctrinal divisions of many Christian denominations. The lowest point in life helped me deconstruct and reconstruct my belief system, faith, and values.

Since then, no one has needed to persuade or convince me for or against my faith in Christ and the path of discipleship in humility, obedience, loyalty; demonstrating through genuine care and kindness to others. I see it as a transformation for me from the inside out.

You see, the difference between being a "fan" and being a "follower" is simple: A fan can jump, and shout sing the proverbial national anthem just like you see at football matches all over the country.

But being a follower? That's someone who is committed, understands the cost and risks of following Jesus. In Mark 8:34 Jesus said "if anyone wants to follow me, let them deny themselves and take up his cross and follow me"

DAVID ANDREW

YOUR THOUGHTS:

BUSINESS

2. Our belief or unbelief doesn't determine the existence of God.

No one can prove or disapprove of the existence of God. God himself says no one has seen him, and he revealed himself by sending his Jesus Christ to humanity in the flesh. Numerous passages in the Bible confirm the existence of God, and there are many examples found in the Bible.

Jesus said to him, "Have I been with you for so long a time, and you do not know Me yet, Philip, nor recognise who I am? Anyone who has seen Me has seen the Father. How can you say, 'Show us the father?' John14:9

God is a spirit [the source of life, yet invisible to humankind], and those who worship Him must worship in spirit and truth." John 4:24

To believe is innate within us. The truth is, we choose what we want to think or not.

DAVID ANDREW

YOUR THOUGHTS:

MINDSET

3. Being double-minded and indecisive brings progress and success to a screeching halt.

That man should not expect to receive anything from the Lord. He is a double-minded man, unstable in all his ways. James 1:7-8.

I understand from experience and others that many people in business, networking and my family circle appear to "sit on the fence" instead of making clear solid decisions. They dither and perhaps of fear of loss, uncertainty, or clarity. The danger of being lukewarm is rendering yourself from being practical—Revelation 3:16. So, I will spew you out because you are lukewarm (spiritually useless) and neither hot nor cold.

For anyone to be successful in life, the only way forward is to jump off the fence, be clear and decisive and work. If needed, change your strategies along the way.

DAVID ANDREW

YOUR THOUGHTS:

PRACTICAL

4. Having faith or not is a personal choice. The application determines an outcome

Having faith in yourself or God is a good thing. Faith is an indicator to step forward into action. You cannot rely on anyone's faith in you. Others place their faith in you when you show them you make things happen. People gain trust by your actions and the outcomes. I believe and have faith in God and the ability he has gifted me. I work on my improving my skills to get better results. That's like having total faith in your existence with a purpose and goal to achieve.

DAVID ANDREW

YOUR THOUGHTS:

MINDSET

5. To make the world a better place starts with you.

I love this insight, and there's a good reason for it. I grew up in a blame culture, and I often blamed others for my mistakes, relinquishing personal responsibilities. However, we all want to live in a better world. It means to have great relationships, a better career, and overall better life. Instead of focusing on fixing others, focus on yourself. Set a good example to those around you, and it will slowly but surely create a positive impact. I believe it's better to guide others with your behaviours instead of words. Your children learn more from watching you.

PRACTICAL

DAVID ANDREW

YOUR THOUGHTS:

6. Respect yourself and others and live in peace.

The reason behind this insight is promoting self-respect and respect for others. Growing up in India, culturally, we learn to respect elders very young. And I believe those values stuck with me. Social construct accepts us to be respectful. However, self-adoration and admiration can cloud our judgement in respecting others and, along the way, lose it for ourselves. We all desire to live a peaceful life. But there's a small price to pay respect towards yourself, others, your surroundings, and the environment.

DAVID ANDREW

YOUR THOUGHTS:

SOCIAL

7. Don't blame others for your mistakes. It could become a stumbling block to your maturity and responsibility in adulthood.

I hit rock bottom because of my mistakes. I wanted other people to share the blame. I found reasons to justify my mistakes that wrecked my life. Of course, I learnt valuable lessons and changed several things in life that were not fit for purpose and did not help.

Not taking personal responsibility and blaming others becomes a stumbling block to growing as a mature person. There are several adverse side effects to the quality of life. Think about it!

DAVID ANDREW

YOUR THOUGHTS:

SPIRITUAL

8. Before criticising others, examine your shortcomings. Work on them; it could take a lifetime.

It's an insight to help you be introspective. We all have faults, and sometimes we sweep them under the carpet. Undoubtedly it collects there. However, when we criticise others, you'll be surprised that it is directly coming from under your carpet when you blame others. "Under the carpet" is like your subconscious, and it surfaces it evokes when provoked. Hypocrisy comes back to bite. There's a great saying from the Bible:

"Why do you look at the speck of sawdust in your brother's eye and pay no attention to the plank in your eye? You tell brother, let me take the speck out of your eye,' when all the time there a plank in your eye? You hypocrite, first take the plank out of your sight, and then you will see clearly to remove the speck from your brother's eye." Matthew 7:3-5

DAVID ANDREW

YOUR THOUGHTS:

PRACTICAL

9. Before you offer solutions to people's problems, make sure it has solved yours.

PRACTICAL

DAVID ANDREW

YOUR THOUGHTS:

PRACTICAL

10. You Can Be Humble & Strong WITHOUT being timid or meek. Just Because You're Humble Doesn't Mean You're Weak.

People have told me that I'm a very humble person.

And even though I didn't start off that way, over the past 10 years or so, I would say my humility and humbleness is one of my strongest assets, as that's allowed me to connect and engage with different people from all walks of life.

The people and cultures might be different, but humility and kindness that EVERYONE – regardless of background – understands, and usually positively responds to.

I say "usually" because that's not always the case.

Sometimes I find that people mistake my humbleness for weakness.

They think that just because I'm a "nice guy" and a giving person, that I can be easily duped or taken advantage of. And that couldn't be further from the truth.

You can be the type of person who considers the needs of others first, while also speaking up for your own needs or desires in life or business.

You can be the type of person who goes out of their way for others and commits "random acts of kindness" to make their lives easier, while also taking care of yourself.

You can be the type of person who does NOT need to overinflate their own self-worth and exaggerate their

DAVID ANDREW

YOUR THOUGHTS:

PRACTICAL

accomplishments, while also being confident in your ability to move forward and get stuff done.

For whatever reason Western society leads people to believe that it's a binary choice: You can either be big and strong, or kind and meek and that simply isn't the case.

As a matter of fact, as someone who has tried both, I would say that it is MUCH easier to move yourself forward while in the process of helping others.

In other words, to be focused on what you're trying to do in your life or business, WHILE being cognizant of how you can help others along the way.

Maybe you notice someone at the store or along your travels who looks like they could use a little "pick me up". What difference would it make to spend 30 seconds giving them some words of encouragement, THEN continuing with your day?

Or maybe you're a business owner and you decide to give someone a little "extra service" for whatever reason...a gift, free shipping...whatever the case maybe. Does giving away those extra few pounds really impact your business' overall profitability that month?

Probably not. Yet think of how happy that unexpected "extra" something could have in someone's life.

DAVID ANDREW

YOUR THOUGHTS:

SPIRITUAL

11. Be Strong as a Lion, but Gentle as a Dove

As a businessperson I've run into all kinds of people: People who were super nice, people who weren't and everyone else in between.

And one of the things I've noticed is that when I'm talking to someone who I would consider arrogant or just super focused on their own needs, I'm almost always unimpressed.

Why?

Because while talking to those people I usually find myself feeling deflated or talked down to.

You ever have that?

People who to feel better about themselves, they try to make you feel worse about yourself.

And it's not like they do it on purpose per se, they just don't know any other way to communicate. But when I run into someone who is simultaneously confident in themselves (strong as a lion), but is also a genuine, caring person (gentle as a dove), then I feel MUCH different.

I feel empowered.

I feel uplifted.

I feel motivated.

And not because they're Tony Robbins, but because they are modelling a behaviour that I want to have

DAVID ANDREW

YOUR THOUGHTS:

SPIRITUAL

more of in my own life, and in that process, motivating me to step into my more empowered self.

Versus talking at me and putting me down, to feel better about themselves.

I met many people who are arrogant for apparent reasons. I couldn't figure it

out. They do not make you feel good if you are around them. And if you feel

humiliated or afraid, don't act timid. Instead, approach humility and be

assertive to voice your thoughts.

Begin by asking a question, and I still do.

"With a gentle smile, say hello; sorry may I interrupt you for a second?" Be bold

and assertive as a lion and state your case in a soft voice and stop. Don't stare

at that person, instead, soften your gaze, lessening the smile. Try doing this in

front of a mirror until you feel comfortable. Over time, you will feel

courageous and yet humble.

It's a balancing act. With practice, you can master it!

DAVID ANDREW

YOUR THOUGHTS:

SPIRITUAL

12. I may not remember everything I've said and done. But it is recorded and plays back through my behaviours and lifestyle. God's Book of Life records everything I've ever done.

DAVID ANDREW

YOUR THOUGHTS:

MINDSET

13. If someone judges you for actions and behaviours and it offends you, they could be right or wrong. But if you do self-soul-search, you have your answer.

A valuable lesson to learn, we all subconsciously naturally judge others, and it happens in seconds. Our First thoughts are first thoughts, and if we do not have a few moments to recalibrate our responses, it's easy to offend when we don't mean it. However, if the offended person questions your remarks, explain your reasons gently to understand you better. If you have genuinely offended someone, seek forgiveness, and make up and move on.

DAVID ANDREW

YOUR THOUGHTS:

MINDSET

14. Humility and meekness don't mean timidity and weakness. Imagine yourself as strong as a lion and gentle as a dove.

I met many people who are arrogant for apparent reasons. I couldn't figure it out. They do not make you feel good if you are around them. However, if you feel humiliated or afraid, don't act timid. Instead, approach humility and be assertive to voice your thoughts. Begin by asking a question, and I still do. "With a gentle smile, say hello; sorry may I interrupt you for a second?" Be bold and assertive as a lion and state your case in a soft voice and stop. Don't stare at that person; instead, soften your gaze, lessening the smile. Try doing this in front of a mirror until you feel comfortable.

Over time, you will feel courageous and yet humble. It's a great balancing act. With practice, you can master it!

DAVID ANDREW

YOUR THOUGHTS:

MINDSET

15. Words have the power to hurt and to heal. How will you speak to yourself and others?

Contrary to the nursery rhyme, Sticks and Stones won't break my bones, but words will never hurt me. This rhyme was in the context of preventing bullying fights at school.

When words are said in jest, sarcastically, snidely remarks and innuendos can often hurt people deeply and etched into memories haunting them.

In contrast, kind and encouraging words will empower and build confidence. You can destroy someone's spirit with one nasty and vindictive remark. If the listener is sensitive will hurt quickly.

Remember, negative self-talks are destructive and dangerous and send some down a vicious circle.

DAVID ANDREW

YOUR THOUGHTS:

SPIRITUAL

16. Whether you pray or not, someone is praying for you. Jesus intercedes to His Father on your behalf.

SPIRITUAL

DAVID ANDREW

YOUR THOUGHTS:

SPIRITUAL

17. Sin is not just about doing bad things. Sin is unwilling to admit that we have the capability of doing bad things. More so, missing the mark by a mile.

DAVID ANDREW

YOUR THOUGHTS:

SPIRITUAL

18. Hardening our hearts against God's love is the beginning of the decay of the soul.

SPIRITUAL

DAVID ANDREW

YOUR THOUGHTS:

SPIRITUAL

19. God's invisible, but you hear about Him from many religions. Some call Him a higher conscious being, the universe, more significant force, and anything else. With different perspectives on God, what is about God that enriches life?

I believe there's one God, and He is the creator of the universe. Genesis 1:1 In the beginning, God created the heavens and the earth. Now is the opportunity to enrich our lives by believing in God and building a relationship with Him in love and humility. What alternatives do you pursue if not this one?

DAVID ANDREW

YOUR THOUGHTS:

MINDSET

20. Being ignorant of truth or lie is like burying your head in the sand and saying the sun doesn't shine.

You are familiar with the cliché "Ignorance is Bliss". You can look at it in two ways. You say to yourself, I don't know about it, so there's no need to worry, essentially ignore it. You choose not to deal with it or take responsibility. In the short term, it might appear bliss.

The other way is to understand what you don't fully understand, become aware of it, and deal with it appropriately. That way, you learn much more than you think to become better, more responsible, and wiser.

DAVID ANDREW

YOUR THOUGHTS:

SPIRITUAL

21. If you are an atheist, you have nothing more to say – A – Theist means there's no God or God doesn't exist. Therefore, debating about someone who doesn't live is a senseless and pointless endeavour. Perhaps it's more meaningful to talk about the Wormholes or the String Theory.

The philosophical argument presented by the seventeenth-century French philosopher, theologian mathematician, and physicist Blaise Pascal posits that human being's wager with their lives that God either exists or does not. Pascal argues that a rational person should live as though God exists and seek to believe in God.

And that makes sense. But here's the thing: The belief in God is an exercise in FAITH and MORALITY rather than just logic.

Is it "logical" to believe in God?

It's natural for humans to be rationale and logical – For example, we don't step in front of fast-moving lorry on a busy highway. We know how to stop when we see a red traffic light. We apply rationale and logic practically to all situations.

But we don't recognise, that we are also applying faith and belief in a system that causes us to behave in a logical way.

SPIRITUAL

DAVID ANDREW

YOUR THOUGHTS:

SPIRITUAL

Believing and having faith is constitutes human personality. A baby displays belief and faith without being able to articulate. The mother knows what to do when a baby cries.

As Pascal quotes "There is a God shaped vacuum in the heart of every man which cannot be filled by any created thing, but only by God, the Creator, made known through Jesus."

To accept God with the fear of him inviting you to heaven or banishing you to hell is not the only reason. Redemption of humankind is close to God's Heart.

We must seek to find truth and evidence through God's word, The Bible, the book that continues to stand the test of time, archaeology, historical and scientific facts. Anything less is short-sightedness.

Ultimately, it boils to personal conviction and interpretation: That's the choice we're always left with, no matter what happens.

DAVID ANDREW

YOUR THOUGHTS:

PRACTICAL

22. Why do some people do well while others don't? There are two possible reasons:

The ones who do well are committed, consistent and give no excuses.

The ones who are neither committed nor consistent with those who do.

PRACTICAL

DAVID ANDREW

YOUR THOUGHTS:

MINDSET

23. Don't waste your time by minding other people's business. There could be many unfinished tasks in your business.

DAVID ANDREW

YOUR THOUGHTS:

PRACTICAL

24. Improve the quality of your mental health

Read and write 500 words every day.

Spend at least 30 minutes in prayer and reflective thinking, and mediation

Minimise the use of intelligent devices and glaring at the TV screen.

I believe in reading, writing, listening, and learning every day from various sources. I call it mental gymnastics. If you daily exercise the brain with helpful information, comprehend and use it wisely; mentally, you feel productive, fulfilling and accomplishing. Moreover, there's always something new to learn and improve.

DAVID ANDREW

YOUR THOUGHTS:

BUSINESS

25. You cannot control time, but you can waste by your actions or lack it.

The cliché Time is Money makes sense if someone makes money within that timeline. Think differently! Time and space go hand in hand. You have the time to breathe find space to explore opportunities that often pass without noticing them. Consider time as priority productivity, not a resource you can squander off.

If time is money and means earning money, then no matter what you do, if you spend more than the required time for the job, you are wasting time and losing money and energy. In one of the meetings, a CEO of the largest council in Europe once said, "Endeavour to get it right the first time," and his words stuck with me today. Time is abundant, and you can manage your tasks within the time you allocate.

DAVID ANDREW

YOUR THOUGHTS:

PRACTICAL

26. If you want to live a peaceful life, there are two things you can do two things:

Stop moaning and complaining.

Forgive yourself and others.

DAVID ANDREW

YOUR THOUGHTS:

RELATIONSHIP

27. If you love someone and they don't love you, you back.
Two things happen:

You can love, and it occurs naturally.

Maybe their perception to love is different to yours.

DAVID ANDREW

YOUR THOUGHTS:

RELATIONSHIP

28. Is it possible to love someone unconditionally? My answer is No, and Why? Because reciprocity is innate, and if not replenished, it empties and dries out when there's nothing left to give.

DAVID ANDREW

YOUR THOUGHTS:

SOCIAL

29. Entitlement is a concept inbred into the modern generation, and you can't blame them. The reason could be parental and societal nurturing.

I raised two boys who are grown up and in their late twenties and early thirties, independent and capable of taking care of themselves and family.

A child's "selfishness" is innate and sharing with others is paternally taught. It's the same in the animal kingdom. However, entitlement is not a millennial mindset...it's something many adults demonstrate as well, but just in a much different way than their younger counterparts.

Entitlement means you have the right to have something if someone has promised you. However, it doesn't mean you automatically get what you want because you want it now by demanding from parents and society.

Instead, I believe in the principle of sowing and reaping. A farmer sows to reap a harvest.

If you haven't sown anything into the society, don't accept to reap anything either. Even worse, you demand someone else's harvest simply because you feel you must have it.

Something for millennials or anyone else to think about, your past mentality has brought you this far. But you can change the trajectory for the better by renewing your mind and empowering yourself with the skills and talents you possess. Aim to upskill and upgrade. You'll feel proud of your achievements.

DAVID ANDREW

YOUR THOUGHTS:

MINDSET

30. The lines blur across a good and a bad life. It is an exchange of perception felt by the one who experiences it.

DAVID ANDREW

YOUR THOUGHTS:

SOCIAL

31. If you ill-treat animals, the likelihood is that you'll ill-treat humans. If you treat animals well, that does not mean you'll treat humans well. Humans can be malicious, whereas animals act instinctively.

DAVID ANDREW

YOUR THOUGHTS:

BUSINESS

32. Not everyone can be a scholar. But everyone can learn to develop a scholarly attitude.

By definition, a scholar is well schooled and advanced in learning, highly qualified and specialises in a particular field of discipline with a PhD degree. Of course, not everyone is educationally highly skilled, and it's not a disadvantage; however, everyone can develop an attitude and mindset of a scholar. Read as much as you can, learn from every mistake and success, be teachable, and do not reject wise counsel or advice. The more you are willing to learn, and you can develop an attitude of a scholar's mindset.

DAVID ANDREW

YOUR THOUGHTS:

SOCIAL

33. Focus on upgrading your skills; the chances are you will get better at what you do.

An analogy. If you are someone like me who travels a lot, especially on planes, travelling in a business or first class is a dream. If you can afford the high astronomical fare financially, then if some force you to downgrade to economy class, it would be unacceptable to you. By a stroke of luck, I got a free upgrade to business class on a few occasions. I was overjoyed and experienced the comfort and hospitality difference between economy and business class flying on a long-haul flight to China. However, one doesn't need to upgrade and fly business or first class to experience the true meaning of upgrading personal skills, talents, and the willingness to be the best one can be. I call this upgrade for life walking the path of excellence.

DAVID ANDREW

YOUR THOUGHTS:

PRACTICAL

34. If you want your children to be model citizens, let them model you.

Anyone can become a biological father and mother to their children. As a parent and experiencing the challenges of raising two children were filled with fun and frustration, but a huge learning curve. I love what the book of Proverbs 22:6 says, "Train a child in the way he should go, and when he is old, he will not turn from it." It talks about your responsibility to lead your child on the right path as a parent.

DAVID ANDREW

YOUR THOUGHTS:

SPIRITUAL

35. Do not lie or exaggerate because the truth will find you out.

It's natural for humans to lie, exaggerate or economise the real thing. In other words, the truth as it happens.

Why? Let's tackle it!

A few reasons

Protect oneself and avoid negative repercussions; Save face; embarrassment, and humiliation; gain sympathy, approval and praise or seek attention. I love what the Bible says in John 8:32, "You will know the truth and the truth will set you free." When questioned, the law requires us to be truthful, so do our parents, educational institutions, employers, and society. So, if the truth is what we want, why lie?

The truth that will set you free is the answer.

Free from guilt, even when we do wrong, admit it, and face the consequence, judgment, punishment, or forgiveness, it will be empowering and experience peace to know that it resulted from being truthful instead of lying. Because it's the truth that set's us free from the prison of our minds.

DAVID ANDREW

YOUR THOUGHTS:

MINDSET growth

36. Practice with a purpose so you know what to accomplish.

In schools, institutions and homes, teachers, coaches, and parents encourage us to practice a particular subject, task, sport, music every day if we are naturally talented or want to get very good at it and then achieve our goals and ambitions.

Practice means doing something repeatedly until it becomes embedded in our minds and muscle memory. However, if there's no purpose to practice, the emotional connection with that objective dissipates because there is no outcome or a result to look forward to and celebrate. Practice with a purpose is also defined as deliberate practice, and it has five critical defining points. Push beyond comfort; define specific goals, intensify the focus; respond to feedback and develop a mental model. One vital thing to remember; is if you aim to be the best at who you want to be and what you decide to do? Then mean it and go for it with all resources at your disposal. No one wants to eat a half-baked cake!

DAVID ANDREW

YOUR THOUGHTS:

BUSINESS

37. You want to achieve goals. Think and be realistic before you set them? Otherwise, they are just pipe dreams.

DAVID ANDREW

YOUR THOUGHTS:

PRACTICAL

38. Speak words that you genuinely mean; otherwise, it's just a noisy chatter.

PRACTICAL

DAVID ANDREW

YOUR THOUGHTS:

PRACTICAL

39. Do not be seduced by glamour, glitter, or people. They can cloud your judgement and leave you confused and at a loss.

PRACTICAL

DAVID ANDREW

YOUR THOUGHTS:

RELATIONSHIP

40. If you immediately get attracted to someone or something and decide to go with it. It indicates a red flag. Red means - Stop! Take time, reflect, and make an informed and wise decision. In the long run, it will save many tears

RELATIONSHIP

DAVID ANDREW

YOUR THOUGHTS:

MINDSET

41. You can't travel in two boats at the same time. Choose one and go the distance. Or else you will drown.

DAVID ANDREW

YOUR THOUGHTS:

MINDSET

42. Everyone is allowed to change their mind. How many times will you change? Imagine, ultimately, what you want and what you get? It might be two different things.

DAVID ANDREW

YOUR THOUGHTS:

MINDSET

43. Being decisive is a sign of being courageous about your conviction; you go with it and deal with the consequences. No one wants to hang around indecisive people.

MINDSET

DAVID ANDREW

YOUR THOUGHTS:

MINDSET

44. If you feel confused, stop, listen to your heart, take a step of faith, and slowly move forward.

DAVID ANDREW

YOUR THOUGHTS:

MINDSET

45. Your past has brought you to your present, and you cannot change your history. Learn some lessons and start moving towards building a better future.

MINDSET

DAVID ANDREW

YOUR THOUGHTS:

PRACTICAL

46. Gossip is juicy but toxic; avoid it at all costs; it will leave you feeling miserable in the end.

PRACTICAL

DAVID ANDREW

YOUR THOUGHTS:

SPIRITUAL

47. If you love to gain knowledge, seek wisdom to help you use it.

Someone said knowledge is power!

Well, it depends on how you interpret it and apply it.

When you possess a piece of vital information that gives an advantage over everyone else, you can feel powerful. However, having power doesn't make one powerful. Power is power. The ability to act on knowledge is power. Most people in most organisations cannot work on their learning; hence, just the knowledge might seem ineffective. To be highly effective and productive, I believe knowledge and wisdom go hand in hand. Knowledge is the information you learn, and wisdom is the ability to use that knowledge profoundly. So, knowledge is a part, and wisdom is the whole. Wisdom goes beyond possessing facts and information; it includes making sense of those facts.

I love what it says in the book of Proverbs 4:7

Get wisdom, get understanding; do not forget my words or swerve from them. Do not forsake wisdom, and she will protect you; love her, and she will watch over you. Wisdom is supreme; therefore, get insight. Though it costs all you have, get understanding.

DAVID ANDREW

YOUR THOUGHTS:

PRACTICAL

48. If someone lies to you, and later you discover the truth, naturally, you feel bad and possibly betrayed. Instead of dwelling on it, let it go. It's very likely that person lies to others too.

PRACTICAL

DAVID ANDREW

YOUR THOUGHTS:

PRACTICAL

49. People are bound to offend you, and probably you will offend others. The fact is that humans cannot always be correct. But if you think before you speak, honour, and stay true to your words, you will offend fewer people.

In today's world, it's impossible not to be offended by someone, something or via the media.

However, we can protect our hearts and minds and harness our emotions from uncontrollable outbursts of anger and anguish. It's vital to understand and embed in our mindset; there will be many things outside our control like we cannot stop the sun from shining or the rain to fall. We can only control the heat burning us and the water drenching us wet.

Our emotions, words and actions are within our control; we'll have a fine day when we learn to harness it and execute it wisely.

PRACTICAL

DAVID ANDREW

YOUR THOUGHTS:

SOCIAL

50. In life, you cannot please everyone. If you try and please everyone, eventually, you will lose your authenticity. Pursue what's good for you, then you will feel good about yourself.

DAVID ANDREW

YOUR THOUGHTS:

MINDSET

51. If you permanently settle for the second-best, second best is always what you'll get.

MINDSET

DAVID ANDREW

YOUR THOUGHTS:

PRACTICAL

52. If you are always busy,
    then consider measuring your
    productivity.

PRACTICAL

DAVID ANDREW

YOUR THOUGHTS:

SOCIAL

53. Before you say yes to someone, count the cost you levy on yourself. Letting others down is embarrassing and shameful. People won't trust you, and you lose their respect.

We live in a world where people want to please other people. There are many reasons to please someone; maybe you want something in return or impress or make them feel good. So we say YES to things even when we want to say NO. Mostly in the workplace and from personal experience, it's difficult to say No to the boss, so one ends up saying Yes. It's good to be truthful and deal with the outcome. It will empower you.

It's essential to recognise that it's vital to follow up and do it once we give our word to someone because the negative impact is loss of trust, potentially relationships. No one will take that person seriously if it happens repeatedly.

DAVID ANDREW

YOUR THOUGHTS:

MINDSET

54. Bravery is not about fighting everyone. It is about adhering to your values and principles and living by them.

MINDSET

DAVID ANDREW

YOUR THOUGHTS:

SPIRITUAL

55. Don't shut the door on receiving wisdom. Because in the land of fools, everything is parched and dry.

SPIRITUAL

DAVID ANDREW

YOUR THOUGHTS:

BUSINESS

56. Success is not only measured by what you achieve. It is also measured by when you help others succeed.

There is no shortage of answers. But deciding how you will define, and measure success is one of the essential exercises you can ever do.

My definition of success is simple; it was a shift in my paradigm of seeing success before and how I see it now. Before it was a desire to be wealthy by trying many ways of earning money, dreaming of living in a big house, expensive cars, designer clothes, luxury holidays, and I could list numerous desires and wants money could buy.

For many, that definition of success materialised but not for me. I realised if I had everything money could buy but never realised some things I would be missing—my peace of mind, remarkable physical, mental, spiritual health, emotional stability, contentment, a meaningful relationship, and longevity. Many may not consider it as being "successful". I learned that even achieving the new paradigm of success wasn't easy. Still, I began to pursue it with all my being, and it took several years before I began to experience the taste and meaning of success according to my definition.

Now, I help many others achieve what I have achieved. And helping others along that path and seeing them become successful is a greater reward and trustworthy success for me.

DAVID ANDREW

YOUR THOUGHTS:

57. If you are in debt because you don't understand the value of your possessions, neither do you know how to manage money. Easy come, easy go!

DAVID ANDREW

YOUR THOUGHTS:

PRACTICAL

58. Generosity is a sign of abundance. Meanness displays poverty.

Generosity and Meanness are the two sides of the same coin. Just imagine you have a friend who's always first to pull out his wallet to pay for a round of drinks and think of a friend who often forgets his wallet and even he doesn't wait for someone to pay first. Generous people are happier and enjoy giving without expecting anything in return. Mean people feel miserable because they go without many things and are worried about losing what they have. It's true; wealthy people can be equally stingy and mean. Generosity is a heart attitude, and so is Meanness.

DAVID ANDREW

YOUR THOUGHTS:

BUSINESS

59. When greed takes over our lives, nothing will satisfy that greed.

BUSINESS

DAVID ANDREW

YOUR THOUGHTS:

MINDSET

60. If you want to win someone's heart, first, you must win your own.

DAVID ANDREW

YOUR THOUGHTS:

PRACTICAL

61. Confidence is not arrogance, but arrogance demonstrates weakness.

Confidence and arrogance stem from one's belief in oneself; however, arrogance results from an exaggerated sense of self, egoistic, bold, and aggressive.

That person tries to overpower others in an intimidating way—the roots of such behaviour deep down to insecurity and low self-esteem. Such people demonstrate narcissistic tendencies.

A confident person works hard, hones their skills, becomes excellent at whatever they decide to do, and feels proud of their achievements and top it with humility, like icing on the cake.

DAVID ANDREW

YOUR THOUGHTS:

MINDSET

62. Confidence develops your ability to do your best without comparing yourself with someone's best.

"Optimism is the faith that leads to achievement. Nothing can be done without hope and confidence." **Hellen Keller**

There's an irony about becoming confident by comparing yourself with others—the irony of comparing oneself with others to beat them down and show yourself better. I believe jealousy plays a part in it, and once jealously takes hold, it builds into bitterness and resentment. One must stop comparing oneself with others in that way.

Instead, become the best you can be and learn to become Content with what you truly achieve. Your hard work, dedication and commitment will pay off well. Remember, you can never out compare yourself with someone; our planet is enormous and clocking 7.8 billion people and growing; there's bound to be someone better or worse off than you.

Keep doing your best each day and measure it against your best yesterday. Because tomorrow you'll have another opportunity to be better.

DAVID ANDREW

YOUR THOUGHTS:

BUSINESS

63. When you stop learning, you stop growing.

DAVID ANDREW

YOUR THOUGHTS:

SPIRITUAL

64. When you spend most of your time on self-interest and self-admiration, the chances are you miss out on other valuable things around you.

DAVID ANDREW

YOUR THOUGHTS:

PRACTICAL

65. If someone upsets, you without your provocation. Remember, it's not your problem but theirs, in which case, ignore, forgive, and move on.

PRACTICAL

DAVID ANDREW

YOUR THOUGHTS:

SPIRITUAL

66. If you genuinely want to be wealthy, sow kindness, compassion, and forgiveness seeds. You will reap a bountiful harvest to transform souls in the right season. Potentially the world will be a better place to live.

SPIRITUAL

DAVID ANDREW

YOUR THOUGHTS:

MINDSET

67. If people only love, you because you do things for them. Then perhaps their love for you is not genuine.

DAVID ANDREW

YOUR THOUGHTS:

SPIRITUAL

68. If you say sorry, then mean it and try not to repeat the same mistake.

It's crucial to realise that when you offend someone, the offended person may hurt and feel sad at different degrees depending upon their sensitiveness, healing time, and recovery.

So, when you say sorry and apologise, let them sense your sincerity in your apologies. And if the pain you caused is intense, show remorse. And pray that person forgives you. And when they do, do not offend, and hurt them again. Eventually, your sorriness and apologies will mean nothing if the pattern continues.

I also want to add a spiritual dimension to sorry, apologies using the word repent or repentance asking God to forgive us for our sins. It means reviewing one's actions and feeling contrition or regret for past wrongs, accompanied by a commitment to take steps to show and prove a change for the better.

"If we confess our sins, God is faithful and just to forgive our sins and cleanse us from all unrighteousness." 1 John 1:9

DAVID ANDREW

YOUR THOUGHTS:

PRACTICAL

69. Greed and lust for lifeless objects like material possessions have no intrinsic value until you emotionally attach and place value on them. Your relationship is one-sided by giving you a false sense of security and often leaving a vacuum of feeling empty and isolated.

DAVID ANDREW

YOUR THOUGHTS:

SPIRITUAL

70. If you want true peace of mind? Then declutter your mind from lifeless objects that serve no purpose. And distance yourself from people who zap the life out of you. They are a vexation to your spirit.

To enjoy peace of mind and contentment in the chaotic world is nothing short of almost 'a miracle.'

Very few achieve the peace that surpasses all understanding that Jesus promises. Philippians 4:7. It's that peace I am pursuing, and hence my thoughts on decluttering and distancing from negative people.

Peace is abstract and often misunderstood by many, equating to possessing materialist things the world offers. I have nothing against material possessions. We all need some form of material possessions to survive, live and meet our daily needs. However, it's easy to cross the fine line between having material goods and being emotionally attached and hoarding. If you lose them, it can destroy peace and contentment very quickly.

It's true that all handmade, manufactured objects are lifeless and do not breathe, eat, or live. If you do not use them for days or decades, they collect dust, and some even deteriorate and depreciate, often left abandoned or someone inherits them.

DAVID ANDREW

YOUR THOUGHTS:

SPIRITUAL

Likewise, if you value your peace of mind, keep away from living objects such as people who emit negative energy, toxic and coarse conversations, and fluctuating mood swings. They offer nothing to uplift your soul or inspire; instead, they zap everyone's energy mentally and emotionally, robbing others of joy and peace.

I love the poem Desiderata by **Max Ehrmann**, *and one of the lines reads, "Avoid loud and aggressive persons, they are vexations to the spirit." If you compare yourself with others, you may become vain and bitter, for always there will be greater and lesser persons than yourself.*

Enjoy your achievements as well as your plans.

DAVID ANDREW

YOUR THOUGHTS:

MINDSET

71. It's more satisfying to have few committed followers on social media who find value in your offerings, implement, and enjoy the benefits instead of millions with whom you have no connection, commitment, or loyalty.

I have followers on LinkedIn, Instagram, Twitter, and Facebook. Compared to some people in the orbit of connection, my count of followers is insignificant. Before, it used to bother me, and I also felt jealous and low about it.

It is important to remember that when your followers find someone better, they'll jump ship and follow them. When someone follows you – it implies you are leading them. So, ask yourself what kind of leader are you and where are you leading them?

DAVID ANDREW

YOUR THOUGHTS:

SPIRITUAL

72. Jealousy is like a slow, painful death; it doesn't kill you right away. However, it is the single most cause of inflicting horrific pain if it engulfs your life. Let it go and live in peace.

SPIRITUAL

DAVID ANDREW

YOUR THOUGHTS:

MINDSET

73. Suffering is incorporated into our lives because it helps shape our character makes us stronger, resilient, and stoic.

DAVID ANDREW

YOUR THOUGHTS:

PRACTICAL

74. To live a healthy lifestyle, nourish your body and nurture your soul.

DAVID ANDREW

YOUR THOUGHTS:

SPIRITUAL

75. Loyalty is earned and not demanded.

*Hollywood actor **Dwayne Johnson** wrote: Blood, Sweat and Respect First two you give. Last one you earn. However, you describe it, loyalty, trust, and respect is a process that demands sacrifices, effort, and consistency.*

Probably, we have experienced two extreme spectrums: gained and betrayed. Perhaps we might have done the same to others.

Loyalty can take time to build by living with integrity ethically and backed with evidence.

So, it's impossible to demand loyalty and respect without having a clean track record of integrity.

Let's build loyalty in every aspect of our lives and our relationships.

DAVID ANDREW

YOUR THOUGHTS:

MINDSET

76. If you find yourself repeating the same mistakes? Pause and ask why? Perhaps you are not learning lessons from them?

MINDSET

DAVID ANDREW

YOUR THOUGHTS:

SPIRITUAL

77. If you have low self-esteem? The chances are someone's told you that repeatedly.

I felt unhappy about everything for years because it wasn't good enough, and others were better than me. Looking back, I learned most of my self-pity was because I nurtured negative comments in my thoughts, whether someone deliberately projected on me or not. I created a picture of myself by allowing others to paint it for me. You must remember it's not you but the projection of their words playing on your life screen, which you must stop and pull the plug on it. Your thoughts create you!

DAVID ANDREW

YOUR THOUGHTS:

PRACTICAL

78. When you create memories, you might cherish them. But if they haunt you, go ahead and delete them.

DAVID ANDREW

YOUR THOUGHTS:

MINDSET

79. If you have regrets, there's a reason. You can overcome the healing process by forgiving yourself and others who played a part in it.

DAVID ANDREW

YOUR THOUGHTS:

SPIRITUAL

80. **If you become angry quickly, you need help, and it's available.**

Try this. Stop, breathe, and count slowly backwards from 10 to 1. If your anger has cooled down, you are in control of your emotions. That is how I overcame immediate outrage.

DAVID ANDREW

YOUR THOUGHTS:

MINDSET

81. Anger is an emotion and if you want to release it, do it properly by talking without shouting. Unleashing anger on someone harms them and you.

MINDSET

DAVID ANDREW

YOUR THOUGHTS:

SPIRITUAL

82. If your mood changes frequently, you make it difficult for others to hang around you. The chances are that people will distance themselves from you. Don't be surprised if you feel isolated. If the problem persists, seek help, and talk to someone who cares enough to help you.

DAVID ANDREW

YOUR THOUGHTS:

MINDSET

83. Many articles are written about "how to have great relationships" and avoid getting into bad ones. But most of us discover it much later.

I have first-hand experience in the highs and lows of a relationship, and I learned from many close friends who experience tumultuous relationships. The easy bit is to blame, but I'm not sure it helps much. Starting any relationship is a decision and commitment between two people who decide to be together. So, be open and truthful about your expectations. It's like the two wheels on a bicycle revolving together. There's never been a perfect relationship – but you can have a fulfilling relationship if you learn to manage each other's expectations.

DAVID ANDREW

YOUR THOUGHTS:

SPIRITUAL

84. Don't advise anyone unless they ask. That person will blame you if it fails to work.

Everyone is entitled to their own opinion. You are, I am... heck, even a dog is entitled to give his own opinion when he barks at a stranger at the door. But the problem with providing a ton of "advice" when it's unsolicited is that people can take that the wrong way or worse yet, they can "take your advice" but execute it in the wrong way, and then hold YOU responsible for their results!

Here's what I say to people if you're trying to lead a peaceful life and want to genuinely help others with your insight or experience... say this instead:

"Boy that sounds like a really difficult situation. And I'm NOT telling you what to do. However, I do have some experience with this that might help, would you like to hear it?"

Now if they say yes, then you tell them. If they say no, then you don't. But what doesn't happen is they feel "put upon" by what you would do in their shoes. Nobody wants to be told what to do, and even the most well-meaning advice can make people feel pressured, stressed or even resentful towards the person giving. Does that mean you don't help people out when you can? Of course not. But it does mean that you go about it in a way that is prayerful and gracious, that gives room for others to accept it or not.

DAVID ANDREW

YOUR THOUGHTS:

MINDSET

85. Everyone is entitled to their opinions, but some are highly self-opinionated.

The difference between giving an opinion and being self- is that wise words can positively impact someone. But being around self-opinionated people may cause others to feel frustrated and resentful.

DAVID ANDREW

YOUR THOUGHTS:

PRACTICAL

86. Treat men, women, and children with dignity and respect. Everyone deserves it. Give respect to gain respect.

Treat people with dignity by showing respect even if you disagree with them. Although gender, age, strength, and vulnerability differentiate us, we are humans. And being kind and respectful to each other can only be a good thing.

Remember, we were once children, and we'll grow old. We are most vulnerable at both ends of the spectrum.

When respecting our differences feeds our thinking, naturally, we'll treat others with respect and dignity. We give respect to gain respect.

Just imagine how life would be with all-round respect. Increased safety for everyone, less stress, and improved relationships can positively impact personal and professional lives.

PRACTICAL

DAVID ANDREW

YOUR THOUGHTS:

PRACTICAL

87. Take good care of the elderly and vulnerable people. They need us, and it's an opportunity to demonstrate humanity.

DAVID ANDREW

YOUR THOUGHTS:

ENVIRONMENT

88. Littering is the bane of our society, neighbourhood, streets, parks, ocean, forest, and the environment. Please stop littering. Please take your litter home and bin it properly.

Many years ago, I developed a strong standpoint against people carelessly and wilfully littering anywhere or everywhere. And till this day and in the future, I will hold that view toward littering less graciously.

I watched local governments doing short term campaigns on Stop Littering in a voice I felt was pussy footing around the subject, gently coaxing people not to litter. I am not sure about the statistical percentage figures on reducing littering. My eyes did not notice a sustainable difference. It's a deep-rooted behavioural change that is difficult to achieve. I suggest learning from the Singaporeans and the Japanese. Singapore is bent on maintaining its reputation of being impeccably clean, with an active campaign against littering and stringent enforcement in place. First-time offenders who throw small items like cigarette butts or candy wrappers get a fine of $300. Not littering has become part of Japan's culture: most Japanese people will take their rubbish home with them rather than dispose of it when out and about.

DAVID ANDREW

YOUR THOUGHTS:

ENVIRONMENT

89. Driving dangerously above speed limits, especially in built-up areas and breaking the law is nothing short of reckless behaviour.

Consider the ramifications; it could wreck a family life. If you enjoy speeding, there are plenty of racetracks to unleash the adrenaline rush– Speed kills. You are responsible behind the steering wheel, irrespective of other drivers on the road. To be a safe driver, learn to manage road conditions and traffic flow and minimise the chance of accidents.

ENVIRONMENT

DAVID ANDREW

YOUR THOUGHTS:

ENVIRONMENT

90. Vehicle parking spaces are for a specific purpose; *single space* for one vehicle. Park correctly with due consideration for other drivers. Do not double park on the streets; it inconveniences other road users and is dangerous.

ENVIRONMENT

DAVID ANDREW

YOUR THOUGHTS:

BUSINESS

91. Running a large or small business; focus on serving your customers well. They are the bloodline of any business.

I am a big believer in making the customer experience the best. Having dealt with large corporations to a corner shop owner, from experience, I learned that either of them can provide high-level customer service and not. The enormous intricacy and bureaucratic processes and systems built into business and people with diverse attitudes and mindsets managing the system can ultimately harm the quality of the service. Finally, the customer suffers who pays for everything. Has this ever happened to you?

You spend the money and buy the product. And then a week later something happens, and you call customer service. Except the "service" you get is more in line with the policies and procedures of the company and essentially how you should have either known better, done something different...but regardless, "No Mr. Customer sorry we can't help, or you can't get your money back?" How did that make you feel? If you're like me, probably frustrated and even a little angry.

But if you're a small business owner (or even part of a larger company), serving your customers well is not only important from a business perspective, but also from a moral one.

DAVID ANDREW

YOUR THOUGHTS:

BUSINESS

So not matter what size business you are, Remember! The customer is the bloodline of your business. If you drive them away, you drive away your income, and earn a bad reputation. It takes a long time build a great reputation, but it can be quickly destroyed - especially in the age of social media and unverified statements.

Is it worth the risk?

"Serve wholeheartedly, as if you were serving the Lord, not people, because you know that the Lord will reward each one for whatever good they do, whether they are workers or volunteers Be known for great leadership and service to your customers, but also to your employees and vendors" .Ephesians 6:7-8 Whatever you do, work heartily, as for the Lord and not for men,

Colossians 3:23

SOCIAL

DAVID ANDREW

YOUR THOUGHTS:

92. Supermarkets are a place generally people from all walks of life shop and rub shoulders. It's up to the store management and staff to provide the best customer service experience. The level of customer service can either enrich or dull the shopping experience.

Supermarkets can be a great place to meet and socialise, allowing your visual, smell and taste senses to explore and discover what the store has to offer. Of course, it's equally important to look after the employees because they are the driving force of business where it matters the most. Happy workers make their customers happy.

"It's all about the customer." **Jeff Bezos** – *Founder of Amazon*

DAVID ANDREW

YOUR THOUGHTS:

SPIRITUAL

93. Forgiveness and Reconciliation versus Revenge and Resentment run parallel. You have the choice to execute one.

Looking back and to this day, I know it's not easy to forgive someone depending on how hurt and offended you feel by them.

Naturally, resentment, anger and even revenge start to bubble and wait for the opportunity to repay. Sometimes anger and revenge erupt instantly.

Of course, we know the consequences are painful and more accentuated, and sometimes the cycle of hurt, revenge and resentment continues.

According to an ancient Chinese proverb, "Resentment is a slow death." In contrast, "To forgive is to set a prisoner free, and discover the prisoner was you." **Lewis B Smedes**

DAVID ANDREW

YOUR THOUGHTS:

94. You are responsible for motivating yourself because resources and opportunities are all around you.

We can find inspiration through many sources. It's vital to be inspired.

I am inspired each day. I consider each day a brand-new day; I wake with an attitude of making my day brilliant and productive come rain or shine. Sometimes it just rains, but my intentional attitude enables me to navigate the day.

Motivation means action! - It means to get yourself out of bed and get ready for the day, energising yourself no matter what it takes without making little and silly excuses.

As an adult, it is your responsibility to motivate yourself no matter what it takes and get into action. Action produces results.

DAVID ANDREW

YOUR THOUGHTS:

PRACTICAL

95. If you are determined to spoil someone's day, ask yourself what kind of day you want to have?

Although we may not intentionally go out to spoil someone's day, we can do it without realising that depending on how we interact with our spouse, colleague, or the community, and it has an effect, either positive or negative.

It's the principle of cause and effect. Cause and effect is the relationship between two things when one thing makes something else happen. For example, if we overeat food and do not exercise, we gain weight. Eating food without exercising is the "cause;" weight gain is the "effect." this is a negative effect. In contrast, when we change the cause, it changes the outcome. If we eat healthily, regularly exercise and maintain a healthy lifestyle, we are less likely to develop long term chronic illnesses and feel good about our bodies, mind, and spirit. We feel joyful and optimistic and more capable of handling unforeseen challenges.

Sometimes we wonder, why is that person feeling bad? What upset them? Perhaps our interaction with them wasn't up to par; we reacted badly without thinking and did not apologise. It's a shame that we can spoil someone's day either intentionally or unintentionally because of careless behaviour, words, and attitude.

However, we can change that. We can intentionally make someone's day happier by

DAVID ANDREW

YOUR THOUGHTS:

PRACTICAL

being pleasant, speaking respectfully and thinking before speaking and reacting.

The responsibility is on us not just to make other people's day great but also our day.

It's a win-win!

A gentle tongue is a tree of life, but its perverseness breaks the spirit. Proverbs 15:4

For "Whoever desires to love life and see good days, let him keep his tongue from evil and his lips from speaking deceit;" 1 Peter 3:10

DAVID ANDREW

YOUR THOUGHTS:

MINDSET

96. If you feel down in the dumps, you can talk to someone who cares about you. You may also, reflect on the root cause and triggers

It's inevitable we have good and bad days. Especially the bad days could be like dark clouds floating across the sun, preventing, or dimming its brightness. It is like having a long bad day if the clouds don't float away, and on top of it, it rain's and gets cold.

We cannot control the sun, the clouds, rain and cold, but we can appreciate the daylight. The sun still shines!

- *There are practical things you can, and experience proved it to work for me.*
- *Sit comfortably with a hot or cold drink.*
- *Take deep breaths, reflect on what is causing you to feel bad, even if it is someone's fault, and it's happened, but you control your thoughts and how to respond.*
- *Take control of your thoughts and reflect without judging others or yourself.*
- *Writing helps! So, take a paper and pen and honestly write down the things that offended and hurt you. Also, write down if your responses were harsh and offensive. Once it's on the paper, it's out of your mind. Close the page, walk around, or go for a walk, sing to yourself, dance if you like or listen to*

DAVID ANDREW

YOUR THOUGHTS:

MINDSET

your favourite music. If you have a dog, take it for a walk. Within a couple of hours or sooner, you'll feel much better. I know it worked and still works for me, and I believe it will work for you.

- *Somethings take longer than others to heal and recover. Healing is a process after hurt.*

DAVID ANDREW

YOUR THOUGHTS:

PRACTICAL

97. You can only do your best. But if you want to do it better, think beyond best.

Even the person who finishes last wants to come first and win the race.

Deep down in our hearts, we aspire to be the best, although, at times, we settle for second best.

The remarkable thing is that we can think and want the best for ourselves, our children, family and friends, and society, and that's excellent!

However, to be the best, you must do the best and the perception you create of being the best.

If you want to improve and go beyond your best, the only way forward is to dedicate, self-discipline and commit your efforts to become better by 1% each day. Practice what you learn and practice more. Measure your progress and compare it with yesterday.

James Clear, *the New York Times's Best Seller of The Atomic Habits, writes that consistently micro-changing bad habits and replacing them with new ones create macro and atomic results.*

DAVID ANDREW

YOUR THOUGHTS:

MINDSET

98. Consider using the word "effortlessly" when you execute any tasks.

I noticed a significant difference overall in my attitude and behaviours. I felt anxiety and stress lessened over time and approached every job, small or big, easy, or difficult, with an attitude of thinking the word "effortlessly". It did not devolve from putting total effort; instead, it harnessed my efforts into upgrading and upskilling everything I do. Then no matter what task you undertake with an attitude of "effortlessness", it changes the paradigm and dynamics of executing the task. Practice it daily, and surprisingly that no matter how difficult the job is, it becomes easier when you approach it with an effortless mindset.

DAVID ANDREW

YOUR THOUGHTS:

SPIRITUAL

99. Your thoughts shape you. Think wisely; what you put in comes out.

SPIRITUAL

DAVID ANDREW

YOUR THOUGHTS:

MINDSET

100. If you want to live longer, healthier, and happier, make it your mission to do everything contributing to the big picture. Life is worth living, and you are in the driver's seat. Build a holistic support system to help you along the journey. You become more competent at managing minor and significant hurdles as and when they crop up.

MINDSET

DAVID ANDREW

YOUR THOUGHTS:

SPIRITUAL

101. Count each day as a gift and a blessing. Even when the clouds appear dark, remember the sun is shining behind those clouds, and you will soon see and feel the difference because the dark clouds do not stay; they float away.

CONCLUSION

I hope you found these insights valuable. Suppose life is a journey, then position yourself in the driving seat and take control of the steering wheel, navigating towards your destination through the ups and downs life throws at you. You may encounter speed bumps, roadblocks, and even breakdowns on this journey. Don't allow the obstacles to threaten you and bring you to a complete halt. Reflect, re-route, stay motivated and keep moving forward.

The experience will be adventurous and have a huge learning curve. And when you finally reach your destination, you will look back and feel proud of the lessons learnt from experiences and say, "it was all worth it".

I hope you found these gems valuable. Embed them in your thought process to help you enjoy your daily life. It will be a learning curve and a pleasant difference to your day.

I would encourage you to write your thoughts and experience the difference it can make for you.

www.ingramcontent.com/pod-product-compliance
Lightning Source LLC
Chambersburg PA
CBHW041214130526
44590CB00061BA/4051